LIBYA
The lost cities of the Roman Empire

Photographs by Robert Polidori

Text by Antonino Di Vita, Ginette Di Vita-Evrard, Lidiano Bacchielli

KÖNEMANN

Acknowledgments

Robert Polidori, the photographer, wishes sincerely to thank the following people, without whom this work would never have seen the light of day. Firstly, Dr. Ali Abdussalem Treki, Ambassador in Paris of the Popular Socialist Libyan Arab Jamahiriyah, for facilitating contacts and opening numerous doors in Libya itself.

Thanks also to Olivier Binst, who looked after the administrative part of the project. His unflagging efforts from the beginning to the end deserve recognition.

Guy Bourreau of Kodak Professional in Paris is warmly thanked for providing the excellent film stock that made the photographs published in this volume possible.

Finally, a special vote of thanks to Ali Emhemmed al-Khadduri and Giuma Anag from the Libyan Department of Antiquities. Mr. Anag spared no effort accompanying the photographer and his assistant Philippe Zeiler on their various missions and removing every obstacle that appeared in their path.

The authors, Antonino Di Vita and Ginette Di Vita-Evrard, also speak on behalf of their late colleague and friend Lidiano Bacchielli, whose last work this is. Their warmest thanks go to the Department of Antiquities of the Popular Socialist Libyan Arab Jamahiriyah. All the staff at the Department, from the Director, who is currently Ali Emhemmed al-Khadduri, to watchmen at the digs have been wonderfully supportive and welcoming over many decades. Thanks to them the authors have been afforded the best possible conditions when working at these wonderful sites.

Thanks also go to Jean-Claude Golvin and GEO magazine for their permission to reproduce four illustrations of Lepcis, including the keys, which they had previously published. The editor made only one change: the removal of people from the drawings.

We would also like to thank Claudio Parisi Presicce and Serenella Ensoli who wrote the keys for the section on Cyrenaica.

PHOTOGRAPHIC CREDITS:
The photographs on pages 14, 28 and 77 (right hand) were taken by Ginette Di Vita-Evrard.

ILLUSTRATIONS
Lepcis Magna: The maps and drawings on pages 47, 61, 68, 77, 92, and 122 are taken from the volume *Lepcis Magna* by R. Bianchi Bandinelli, E. Vergara Caffarelli and G. Caputo (Mondadori), Verona, 1964. The map on page 51 and C. Catanuso's illustration were published by Antonino Di Vita in *La ricostruzione dell'arco dei Severi a Leptis Magna* in *Quaderni di Archeologia della Libia*, 7, 1975 respectively as Fig 29 and an insert. The illustrations on page 118 were taken from *The Severan Buildings of Lepcis Magna. An Archaeological Survey* by J. B. Ward-Perkins (ed. by P. M. Kenrick), Tripoli-London, 1993. The drawings by G. Barozzi of porticoes along the Via Colonnata and in the Severan Forum on page 133 are the property of the "Missione Italiana di Cirene" and first appeared in *Africa Romana*, X, Sassasi, 1994 on pages 708 (article by C. Parisi Presicce) and 723 (article by S. Ensoli Vittozzi) respectively.
Sabratha C. Catanuso's map on page 148 first appeared in an article by A. Di Vita, *Il mausoleo punico-ellenistico B di Sabratha*, in MDAI, *Röm, Abteilung*, 83, 1976. The map on page 152 is courtesy of the British School at Rome and first appeared in P. M. Kenrick's *Excavations at Sabratha 1948–1951*, London 1986.

Cyrenaica: The maps of both Cyrene and Apollonia are taken from R. G. Goodchild's work, *Cyrene and Apollonia, an Historical Guide*, 4th edition, Tripoli, 1981.

Appendixes: (c) Illustration of the site of Lepcis, Jean-Claude Golvin and GEO. The map on page 255 was produced by Valérie Miele.

Illustrations and production: Bela Vista

Design: Bela Vista
© 1998, Édition Mengès

© 1999
Könemann Verlagsgesellschaft mbH
Bonner Str. 126, D-50968 Cologne

Translation from German: Liz Clegg and Peter Snowdon
Editor of the English-language edition: Chris Murray
Managing editor: Bettina Kaufmann
Project coordinator: Jackie Dobbyne
Typesetting: Goodfellow & Egan, Cambridge
Production Manager: Detlev Schaper
Assistänt: Nicola Leurs
Printing and binding for the English edition: Mladinska knjiga, Ljubljana

Printed in Slovenia
ISBN 3-89508-844-7

10 9 8 7 6 5 4 3 2 1

From Zouagha the line of large oases stretching along the shore runs as far as Zenzour, four hours away from Tripoli. Quite close to the very first garden, the ruins of Sabratha, or Abrotunum, lie on the seashore. All I found, alas, was a shapeless maze of debris, among which my eye was caught by sections of some splendid, huge, white marble columns and monolithic cubes, each big enough to fill a cart. I was consoled by copying a Latin inscription from a stele which looked as though it had been carved yesterday. Doubtless the wind had only just uncovered it; we know that the sand is a wonderful preservative of all it buries. On the furrowed cliff my hand scraped on some remarkable mosaic borders. What a harvest there would be here if only excavation were permitted! The kilometer and a half of beach is covered in broken pieces of ashlar, ruined capitals, mosaics, and floors that must have belonged to public places. Luxurious summer houses were dotted along the sea shore, where you can still make out the remains of imposing jetties.

Henri Méhier de Mathuisieulx, *Travels in Tripolitania*, Paris, 1903

ARCHAEOLOGICAL

RESEARCH

IN LIBYA

by Antonino Di Vita

The first archaeological survey of Tripolitania was carried out in 1910 by the Italian archaeologist Federico Halbherr, a celebrated expert on inscriptions who was head of the Italian archaeological mission in Crete. He was accompanied by his colleague Gaetano De Sanctis, a well-known historian. They carried out a reconnaissance of the cities of Pentapolis in Cyrenaica, setting up a base in Benghazi to be used as a permanent Italian archaeological post.

The following year two young scholars (Salvatore Aurigemma, an archaeologist, and Franceco Beguinot, an expert on the Berbers) spent a longer period of time in Tripolitania. It was Salvatore Aurigemma who discovered the first important Christian burial ground, at Ain Zara near Tripoli.

When Tripolitania and Cyrenaica were occupied by the Italians following the Italo-Turkish War of 1911–12, the ancient monuments in the region became the responsibility of an ad hoc service set up within the Italian Ministry for the Colonies, initially coordinated and run by Lucio Mariani. At first this was an adjunct to the Ancient Monuments and Excavations Inspectorate, but later it came under the Superintendency for Tripolitania. The administrative headquarters were later moved to Tripoli. A similar structure was put in place for Cyrenaica, with headquarters in Benghazi.

During the early years of Italian occupation, a number of major finds were made. For instance, there were the discoveries of both the famous statue of Aphrodite found in the Sanctuary of Apollo at Cyrene, and also the Artemis of Ephesus, found in the *sacellum* (shrine) in the amphitheater in Lepcis. In addition, floor mosaics were found in the seaside villa at Zliten and an important neo-Punic burial ground at Forte della Vite in Tripoli. These remains symbolized the presence of three civilizations – Greek, Roman, and Carthaginian – that followed each other and coexisted in the coastal region of what is now Libya.

The outbreak of World War I had immediate repercussions in Libya. Just like the Italian troops, the archaeologists fell back to a few safe cities: Benghazi, Homs, and Tripoli. In fact, in Tripoli it was not so much a case of excavation work as of demolition, carried out against the advice of the Superintendency itself. It was then that the wall that had protected the Barbary city disappeared. From this extensive destruction, however, important facts emerged that contributed to our topographical knowledge of ancient Oea. It also led to the recovery of a great deal of archaeological material that had been reused in medieval structures. During this period, the burial ground in the Forte della Vite was explored; and for the first time extraneous structures were removed from the Arch of Marcus Aurelius and restoration work was carried out on it.

Pietro Romanelli took over from Aurigemma in 1919. He excavated the western outskirts of Tripoli and completely restored the tomb of Aelia Arisuth, famous for its beautiful late-classical paintings. This had already been found as early as 1903 but had then been lost again under the sand.

Romanelli also started exploratory digs in Lepcis that were continued from 1923 by Renato Bartoccini. As

THE TRIUMPHAL ARCH OF OEA

I rounded off the day with a visit to the famous Roman triumphal arch, which is the only thing that survives of antiquity in Tripoli. It is a splendid monument that the natives have turned into a tavern, and though it is half buried beneath the ground, its grandeur still strikes one vividly. Three of the four arches of the building have been bricked in. You can still just about see the façade that remains open, but the others are hemmed in on all sides by stalls and shops. Not even in Rome can you find a triumphal arch made of such gigantic white marble slabs. One asks oneself where such material came from, especially since there are no known marble quarries for miles around. What is even more surprising is to see that there is no mortar holding the slabs in place. Invisible iron hooks are enough to hold this building of over eighteen centuries unshakeably together. It was erected in honor of the emperors Marcus Aurelius and Verus; we know this from an inscription containing their initials. This was the maker's way of commemorating the names of these sovereigns [...] . No one can accuse the natives of having damaged the building. They would not dare rob it of a single stone since a prophecy threatened the most terrible punishments for anyone who tried. According to this prophecy, the whole city would follow the unfortunate into disgrace.

Henri Méhier de Mathuisieulx, *Travels in Tripolitania*, Paris, 1903

Left: Oea (Tripoli). Southwest façade of quadrifrons arch of Marcus Aurelius and Lucius Verus. Through the archway, the port can be seen in the distance. This façade and its counterpart behind are more important than the remaining two since they have niches with statues of the emperors on each side. Over these are male busts (badly preserved) and winged Victories in the corners. The entablature inscription is repeated on all four façades.

Below, left: Oea (Tripoli). Arch of Marcus Aurelius and Lucius Verus, north face of the northeast pier. Unlike the two main façades with their niches, here, between the square pilaster decorated with vine foliage and the pilaster framing the archway, relief work provides the only decoration. From bottom to top: a captive barbarian family, a trophy, and (not visible at the top) the city's tutelary deities in their chariots. The arch, built in solid marble, was commissioned by a rich magistrate C. Calpurnius Celsus. It was inaugurated in A.D. 163–164.

Right: Oea (Tripoli). Marble pediment from the temple consecrated to the colony's local deity, personified by a crowned goddess, or Tyche, seen in the center between two of the city's tutelary deities, Apollo (on the left) and Minerva (on the right). Castor and Pollux, the Dioscuri, stand with their horses at either end (the right-hand figure is not shown). Part of the entablature on this temple was inscribed and the marbles from the temple were found near the arch, in the center of the ancient city. It was built thanks to the generosity of a leading Roman senator who had a successful career. It dates from the start of Commodus' reign (A.D. 183–185).

Bartoccini's funding became more substantial, he began large-scale, well-organized excavation work. This was unquestionably the most important project undertaken by Italian archaeologists between the two world wars. This period in no way neglected the exploration and study of important inland monuments; nonetheless, these were the years when archaeologists concentrated, as was perhaps only natural, on the major ancient cities of the country: in Tripolitania, on Lepcis and Sabratha, which had been buried by sand; in Cyrenaica, on Cyrene and Ptolemais, though Apollonia and Taucheira were not neglected.

The civilizations that were about to be investigated were widely separated not only by the sands of the Sirtican Desert, but also by their totally different cultures. Cyrenaica had been an integral part firstly of Greek and then of Alexandrian civilization. The cities of Tripolitania, on the other hand, were heirs to Carthage, the longest-lived civilization in the region, which lasted until at least the 2nd century A.D. While no one could be ignorant of the former fact, people were indeed unaware of the latter. So it was that in Tripolitania scholars tended to concentrate on later Roman remains, without really bothering about either their earlier Punic origins, or how they had managed to survive through the Byzantine and Arab ages.

In 1928 Bartoccini was replaced by Giacomo Guidi. Under his direction, extensive digging and systematic excavation work continued, and it was he who was largely responsible for unearthing the most important

monuments at Lepcis. At Sabratha he rebuilt the front of the stage in the theater – a colossal task which, despite criticism founded more on romanticism than scientific fact, was in reality a fine example of monumental restoration, using original elements, that both conserved an important site and also provided invaluable information.

When Guidi died suddenly in 1936, the whole of Libya was brought under a single Superintendency of Monuments and Excavations with headquarters in Tripoli, run by Giacomo Caputo. In 1938 the autonomous mission in Cyrene was wound up; established in 1925, this had been run by Luigi Pernier working with Gaspare Oliverio and the architect Italo Gismondi.

For Caputo, and his then assistant Gennaro Pesce, World War II brought the titanic job of trying to protect the region's ancient monuments from the ravages of war. Anything that could be moved followed the retreating Italian troops. This meant that by the winter of 1943, when the British occupied Tripolitania, sculpture from all over the region, even as far away as Cyrene, had been amassed in Sabratha.

The occupying British forces in Libya took over the Superintendency, though they left its technical and scientific running to Italian archaeologists. They did, however, attach Antiquities Officers to it. Three of these officers stand out for the valuable contributions they made to the study of ancient monuments in Cyrenaica and Tripolitania: they were D. E. L. Haynes, J. B. Ward-Perkins, and R. Goodchild. They made sure that the

Superintendency could get on with its work and arrange to have finds displayed in museums near to where they had been discovered. They also looked after necessary restoration work. But above all they were active in the field and started new excavation work, especially J. B. Ward-Perkins and R. Goodchild.

After Libyan independence in 1951, Goodchild became the first Controller of Ancient Monuments in Cyrenaica, which came under the jurisdiction of the new Libyan Department of Antiquities. In Tripolitania the new position of controller was occupied successively by the Italians E. Vergara Caffarelli, from 1952 to 1961, and A. Di Vita, official consultant from 1962 to 1965; then by the Jordanian D. Baramki, and the Iraqi Taha Bakir.

After the war, aerial photography was introduced to archaeological research in Libya. The most outstanding success of this new tool was the discovery of the plan of the ancient town of Euhesperides, right next to Benghazi. Another new means at the disposal of the archaeologists was the Land Rover, a rugged vehicle that opened the way for the systematic exploration of the Jebel uplands and the pre-Saharan regions.

After independence, the whole country developed at an incredible pace, and this meant that archaeological finds came thick and fast. The new Department of Antiquities has tried hard to control the finds and ensure that the most is made of each of them. It has appointed controllers for different regions and employs its own managers and technicians. It has put in place imaginative projects, such as the new museums in Sabratha (the Punic Museum), Tripoli, Lepcis, and Benghazi. Under the direction of Omar Mahjub, it has also funded excavations, such as the work on the wonderful Villa Silin, and also restorations, including the amphitheater in Lepcis.

Foreign missions have also flooded in at the invitation of the Department of Antiquities. This has brought archaeological research in the country to a turning point. Extensive excavation work in large city centers has been replaced by scientifically driven research aimed above all at making already unearthed excavations and monuments accessible to the public.

Today there are a number of reviews dedicated to the subject. These range from *Libya Antiqua* and its *Supplements*, which is the official publication of the Libyan Department of Antiquities, to the Italian *Quaderni di archeologia della Libia* and the related *Monografie*, which have taken over from the old *Notiziario archeologico* (1915–27) and the costly review that used to be published by the Italian Ministry for Colonies called *Africa Italiana* (1927–41). There is also the English publication *Libyan Studies*, published by the Society for Libyan Studies in London. They all report news of scientific projects carried out in Libya each year, both by the Department of Antiquities itself and by foreign archaeological missions and scholars at work there.

Lepcis, Severan Basilica: outer east wall. This picture makes clear how sophisticated the construction of the heavy outer walls was. Here we see the north entrance to the basilica (in the background the carved pillars in the apse of the temple dedicated to Liber Pater). On the ground, white marble Pergamenian capitals lie at the base of their cipolin columns.

Following pages: Lepcis, Severan Forum: looking toward the northeast from the temple area. In the background the high wall of the basilica rises behind openings that were doorways to the small shops running along its side. At either end and in the middle are entrances to the basilica itself. On the ground between the piles of fragments, notice the pattern left by the marble paving stones. For a closer look at the left-hand corner, see page 39.

TRIPOLITANIA

by Antonino Di Vita and Ginette Di Vita-Evrard

THE REGION

In classical times, as today, the stretch of North African coast from the Syrtis Major (the present-day Gulf of Sidra) to Syrtis Minor (the Gulf of Gabès) was nearly all low-lying and almost entirely sandy.

Three ancient cities flourished on this inhospitable coast. Each was situated at the end of a long caravan route winding down through the territory of the Garamantes[1] into the rich heart of sub-Saharan Africa. According to tradition, the three cities had been founded by Phoenician colonists.

Going from east to west, the cities were Lepcis (to which the Romans added the suffix Magna to distinguish it from the city of the same name in Byzacium[2]); Oea, where modern Tripoli now stands; and Sabratha.

It seems that the cities grew up around the sites of seasonal trading posts. The locations had been carefully chosen, as in each case the rocky coast gives way to inlets suitable for ships to drop anchor safely out of the tempestuous prevailing northwest winds.

Lepcis, Oea, and Sabratha therefore had naturally safe harbors and lay at the ends of ancient routes to the south that the presence of primitive trading posts quickly turned into flourishing caravan routes. Moreover, in ancient times the cities enjoyed the benefit of a hinterland that produced major agricultural products, as indeed it could again today.

The cities were, in fact, protected by having the Gefara plain and Jebel[3] hills to their rear, enabling farmers to cultivate valuable crops. The natural shortage of water was overcome by systematically running off water from the wadis (water courses that remain dry for most of the year but then swell to torrents during short rainy seasons). In addition to this farmers also constructed numerous civil engineering works to collect rainwater, and built terraces to retain the thin but fertile humus.

There is no doubt today that the large-scale colonization works that made it possible to grow cereals and olives on the Gefara plain, in the Jebel hills, and throughout a large part of the pre-Saharan area, began when Tripolitania was ruled by the Carthaginians. Literary sources already mention Carthaginian irrigation works along the Cinyps[4] Wadi. They also describe the agricultural bounty of the Emporia[5] region, whose inhabitants were forced by Caesar in 46 B.C. to pay an annual tribute of around one million liters of olive oil. More recently fthe authors have had the results of an archaeological study which discovered that Tripolitania was producing amphorae of olive oil as early as the 2nd to 1st centuries B.C.; the study also discovered oil presses dating from the middle of the 1st century A.D. on farms at the southern end of the pre-Saharan regions. At the same time the find of an ostracon (an inscribed fragment of pottery) from Kussabat, the Msellata capital in the Jebel hills behind Lepcis, has provided proof of Carthaginian farmers and land-owners in a region that today is still one of the best olive-growing areas in the world. In Roman times, agriculture in the area expanded enormously: thanks to the outlet that imperial Rome provided for their goods, the wealth of the three cities on the Tripolitanian coast grew beyond all recognition.

In the 3rd century A.D. a serious crisis sent the economy of the Roman empire into a slump and trade declined sharply; an impact on the Tripolitanian Emporia was inevitable. Neither the measures taken by Emperor Septimus Severus to safeguard the African limes (borders) and the caravan routes, by then a few decades old, nor Emperor Diocletian's measures, which included setting up the provincia Tripolitana (making Tripolitania a Roman province), were able to counter the fact that sea-borne trade was disappearing. Although the process was to take a long time, this marked the beginning of the inexorable decline of the three ancient ports of Tripolitania. They managed to survive the first Arab conquest and beyond, but they had lost their former splendor for ever.

Above: Outskirts of Lepcis: The vertical supports of an oil press. These well-preserved "hewn stones," which litter the countryside for miles around, were mistaken by 18th and 19th century travelers for megaliths.

Opposite: Zliten, Roman seaside villa at Dar Buc Ammera. Floor in opus sectile (inlaid marble) and mosaic panels showing the four seasons (Tripoli Museum). The seasons, a classic motif in Roman mosaics, symbolize the territory's agricultural prosperity.

THE HISTORICAL BACKGROUND

From Carthage to Rome

Were Lepcis, Oea, and Sabratha Phoenician or Carthaginian?

Along the coastline of Libya there is no shortage of promontories where wadis flow into the sea, and there are also many small, habitable islands. Both of these features provided exactly the kind of place that the Phoenicians preferred to settle in. It seems likely that the kind of stop-overs needed by the coastal trade on which Phoenician vessels had been engaged ever since they first sailed west in search of ores must also have existed along the coast of Tripolitania, between the Gulf of Sidra and the Gulf of Gabès. Nevertheless the earliest settlements in the areas where Lepcis, Oea, and Sabratha were to rise have until now provided not a single pottery fragment. It should be remembered, however, that the island of Lide – the rock situated at the mouth of the Wadi Lebdah that was possibly used as an early Phoenician outpost – was completely built over during the construction of the port at Lepcis by Emperor Septimus Severus.

Moreover, archaeological evidence does not tally with references from written sources. The Roman writers Sallust, Silius Italicus, and Pliny the Elder all speak of Phoenician settlements of colonists from Tyre and Sidon in Lepcis; they also maintain that colonists from Tyre settled in Sabratha, and that Phoenicians from Sicily and Africa settled in Oea. Without ruling out the possibility that immigrants from Phoenician cities did at some time move to Tripolitania, we must nevertheless treat these sources[6] with caution.

I think it is legitimate, for instance, to assume that the tradition reported by these late-Roman sources may in part at least have sprung from an understandable local desire to ennoble their own cities by claiming origins that go back as far as possible into the past. In this way they put themselves on a par with the defeated city of Carthage. The Emporia of Tripolitania – fortunate enough to be "free" under Roman rule – also managed to distance themselves from their ancient ties of subjection to the mortal enemy of their new lords, the Romans.

In reality, the growth of trading posts in Tripolitania between the second half of the 7th century B.C. (Lepcis) and the beginning of the 4th (Sabratha) seems directly linked to a specific desire to exploit and augment the natural routes leading into the country's interior. In turn, these led to contacts with the Garamantes tribe, through whom they could tap into the immense resources of sub-Saharan Africa, Cyrenaica, and Egypt. In the late 7th century B.C., this level of economic and political planning could only have been implemented by a power with its own strong trading tradition but with roots already firmly planted in Africa: in other words, Carthage.

The Carthaginians' plan was twofold: on the one hand, they looked toward the Mediterranean; on the other, they sought to dominate Africa. The first treaty they made with the emerging power of Rome in 509 B.C. fits into this scheme of things: under the terms of the treaty, the Romans were prohibited from sailing past Cape Bon (the peninsula at the northeast tip of Tunisia). Another aim of their strategy was to penetrate right to the heart of the Gulf of Sidra. Foundations attributed to the Carthaginians can be found from Macomaca, a busy outpost specializing in salt fish on the Tuaorga Lagoon near Misurata, to Macomades Syrtis and Charax (past present-day Sirte), a town where smuggled Cyrenaican silphium was traded for wine.

These small centers, of which Charax was by far and away the most important, chart the progressive advance of Carthage eastward, toward the point where the celebrated Phileni brothers had died in their attempt to establish a borderline. Although things shifted from time to time under the Ptolemies, this area traditionally

Preceding pages: The market in Lepcis. View of the northwest tholos from the southeast. In the foreground, remains of two small honorary monuments dedicated to local dignitaries. They would originally have borne an effigy of the person in question. Reliefs on the piers of the building to the right suggest that it was originally dedicated to a ship owner (see the illustration at the top of page 20). It was later reused to honor a citizen decorated for "civic merit" after donating four live elephants to the city.

Opposite: Lepcis, the old forum seen from the courtyard of the northwest portico. The "staircase" remains of a wall (left) are of the podium of the Temple to Liber Pater. The height of this podium (note the palm tree next to it) is an important clue as to how tall the buildings were. The fluted white columns date from the time it was rebuilt in the 2nd century A.D.. In the middle of the old forum (top right), are the remains of the Byzantine basilica. Early Phoenician-Punic structures have been located deep under the east side of the piazza. If you imagine them standing (top, to the left of the baptistery), you get an idea of how much history is packed into the area covered in this photograph.

formed the boundary between the Carthaginian African eparchy and Greek-influenced Cyrenaica.[7]

To sum up, all the evidence we have points to the fact that all three Tripolitanian cities – not just the older Lepcis but to a far greater extent the more recent Oea and Sabratha – if they were not colonies of pure Carthaginian origin, at least grew up in a way which suited the plans and needs of that great African power.

Leaving aside the origin of some of the settlements, there seems no doubt that the political and economic name of "Carthaginian colonies" could be applied from the outset to these three cities, (the Emporia) between the Syrtis Major (the Gulf of Sidra) and Syrtis Minor (the Gulf of Gabès).

According to ancient sources, this status was particularly burdensome. We know, for example, that Lepcis paid *vectigal*, or tributes, to Carthage of a talent a day – in other words more than nine tons of silver every year. It is likely that all three cities did the same. So when the Roman general Scipio defeated the Carthaginians at Zama it must have come as a relief to the cities of Tripolitania. Even if after 201 B.C. they still nominally belonged to Carthage, in reality the Emporia of Tripolitania very quickly asserted their independence. Neither the brief domination of Massinissa, king of Numidia, to whom Rome eventually gave the region (probably in about 162–161 B.C.), nor indeed the far more liberal and peaceful rule of Micipsa, held back the development of the three cities. Even though they had to pay tribute to the distant Numidian kings, they preserved their own language, institutions, and religious traditions. But above all they were free to trade on an independent basis.

Today there is irrefutable archaeological evidence that these three cities played a full part in Mediterranean trade. This trade was increasingly dominated by the Romans, and the evidence shows that the Emporia grew progressively richer. Evidence of this is the impressive amount of urban development that took place in Lepcis and Sabratha between the end of the 2nd and the beginning of the 1st century B.C.. In addition, rich Hellenistic cemeteries have been discovered in the suburbs of these two cities as well as in ancient Oea. Mediterranean trade was boosted by ever-growing demand for goods from the inexhaustible resources of the African continent: wild animals and beasts for amphitheaters, hides, ivory, gold dust, semiprecious stones and, of course, slaves. The coastal plain was systematically exploited, making late-Hellenistic Lepcis an important center in the trading of grain. According to the Greek historian Herodotus, the cereal-growing land irrigated by the Cinyps Wadi had very high yields. In addition, sheep farming prospered on the Jebel uplands behind the three cities. Each of these factors, combined above all with the effective independence enjoyed by the cities, soon bore fruit.

Independence: its importance and its effects

Both their geographical position and their legal status as peripheral vassals of the kingdom of Numidia meant that the Tripolitanian Emporia felt no adverse effects from the last Punic War. Lepcis, at least, threw in its lot with Rome from the beginning of the Jugurthine War in 111 B.C., signing a treaty of alliance and friendship. From then on, Lepcis gave its new allies every assistance and in 108 B.C., albeit temporarily, a Roman garrison was stationed in the city. It seems likely that, as during Carthaginian domination, Lepcis continued to function as the administrative capital of the Emporia region. During the 1st century B.C. not just Lepcis but also Oea and Sabratha struck their own bronze coins; Lepcis also had silver coins. The Tripolitanian Emporia remained independent until at least 46 B.C., appearing to escape relatively unscathed from the Roman civil wars: it was in 46 B.C. that Caesar imposed the fine of one million liters of oil as punishment for help given to Juba and Pompey's faction (help which had taken the form of arms, soldiers, and money). We do not know if on that occasion the Tripolitanian cities also lost their legal status as *liberae* (free) cities, only to regain it under Augustus. What is certain, however, is that by the middle of the Augustan era they were autonomous and enjoyed the right to mint coins that bore the likeness of Augustus. For Lepcis, Oea, and Sabratha the increase in traffic and safety on the trade routes into sub-Saharan Africa, the shield provided by Roman troops in relation to the *nationes* (tribes) of the interior, perhaps the lifting of the onerous annual oil tribute that Caesar had imposed, and finally the reconfirmation of a broad measure of independence – all this must have been more than sufficient motive to mint a series of separate coins bearing the head and the symbols of the reigning emperor.

Within the framework of *Africa Proconsularis*, in other words the new Augustan province, the Emporia were more or less left free to govern themselves. Nonetheless, for them too the by-now unstoppable process of incorporation into the Roman empire had begun; it was hastened by the voluntary (and self-seeking) support given by their governing classes to Roman rule.

This had two main effects on the freedom enjoyed by the Tripolitanian Emporia during the 2nd and 1st centuries B.C. First, it established a pronounced degree of political conservatism; second, it opened up the possibility of the Emporia taking over – and this time purely for their own advantage – the trading routes that used to belong to the destroyed city of Carthage.

The limits of the world in which they traded, and clearly in the broader sense also their cultural world, were therefore far greater and more varied than the single Western influence (the Italian peninsula) that the other Carthaginian *civitates* (settlements) of Africa inevitably clung to, whether or not they were free. On the other hand, it is easy to see why the Roman and Italic

Above: Lepcis. The lighthouse on the west quay of the Severan port, eroded by the sea.

Opposite: Lepcis. Paving mosaic in the House of Orpheus, one of the few domus within the town that have been excavated. The frieze shows Orpheus enchanting the animal world with his song. The panels have animal, hunting, and pastoral scenes.

Following pages: Lepcis, the Nilevilla, which stands on the shore between the port and the circus. Detail of a mosaic depicting men fishing on the Nile.

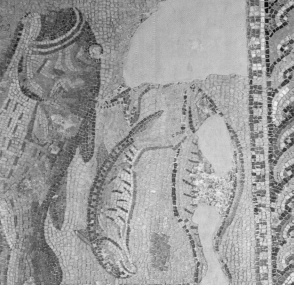

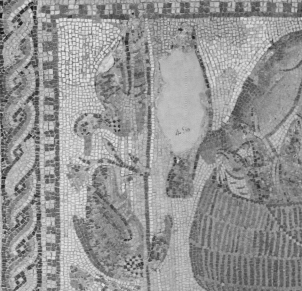

From Constantine to the Arabs

At the start of the 4th century A.D. the Emporia of Tripolitania were shaken by an earthquake that destroyed both Lepcis and Sabratha. (Oea is buried beneath modern Tripoli and so we have no information on this event here.) Houses and monuments alike were flattened, so the inhabitants used the abundance of material made available to build walls around the towns, now much smaller since the outlying districts were abandoned completely. This also shows that they had lost confidence in the Roman army, and that they were under greater pressure from the barbarian *gentes* (tribes) of the interior, anxious to take the well-cultivated land belonging to the coastal cities. At the same time, the grip of central authority was steadily weakening and being replaced by the growing power of local families; as a result, there were also simultaneous changes taking place in the way the cities were laid out. Archaeologists have recently turned up some important results in relation to this. In Sabratha some streets were taken over for private use; powerful family groups gathered, almost certainly not just for convivial purposes, in areas set aside for communal meals next to the tombs of their ancestors. To all this we can also add the spread of small Christian groups.

The French historian Gilbert Picard presumed that the rapid growth of Christianity in Africa between Marcus Aurelius and the Severans was due above all to the demise of the old, pre-Roman Punic rites, and the consequent search for something new with which to replace them. In other words there was a wish on the part of some of the local community, more obstinately attached to Carthaginian culture, not to be swallowed up; even as late as St. Augustine, people in the countryside were still speaking in the Punic tongue. One likely explanation for the rapid integration of what was once Roman Africa into the Arab universe could lie in the common Semitic roots of conquerors and conquered.

In Tripolitania, the earliest traces of Catholic bishops refer to Lepcis and date from the end of the 2nd century A.D. In Sabratha, catacombs of primary importance have also been found, dating from the second half of the 3rd century. But all three cities were deeply divided when the dispute between Catholics and Donatist schismatics was at its height: on more than one occasion the cities had both Catholic and Donatist bishops at the same time.

The Vandals, who favored the latter, finally occupied Tripolitania toward the middle of the 5th century A.D. The three cities, already stricken by a tremendous earthquake in A.D. 365, came under constant threat from tribesmen on camels, such as the powerful Austuriani who reached the heart of Sirtica. They pushed toward the east to pillage Ptolemais and Cyrene, and then to the west, where they laid waste the territories of Lepcis and Oea. Their incursions became ever more ruinous and the cities lost most of their inhabitants.

During the course of the 5th century A.D. and of those that followed, the stable farming populations that had settled inland gradually became more important than those of the coastal cities, deprived as the latter now were of both their hinterland and their trade: at least from the earliest days of the Roman empire up to that time, these had formed the main sources of their wealth.

For example, if we consider Tripolitania in late classical times, we can have no doubt that the Jebel uplands and the pre-Saharan region acquired an importance very different from that which they had had under Carthage or Rome. But by now the world had become very conservative, and in this context the small but secure degree of wealth enjoyed by their communities (a large rural population tending to group together) meant that for the first time in their history these regions were important as a separate economic and social unit. Archaeological research shows that the importance of the regions grew in direct proportion to the progressive decline – irreversible after the turn of the 5th century A.D. – of the coastal cities. Indeed, when the Byzantines arrived, they found only unrecognizable fragments of the past.

In A.D. 533 Belisarius, one of Emperor Justinian's finest generals, was put in command of reconquering Africa: and so in the century in which the Byzantines occupied the three cities of Tripolitania, these cities were living their last moments, not of splendor, but of organized civic life. Sabratha was embellished by a Christian basilica decorated with mosaics of rare beauty; but by now the cities were little more than fortresses. Moreover, the existing religious differences were made even more bitter by the orthodoxy of the Byzantine Church and the Byzantine empire. When Emperor Heraclius died (A.D. 641), while busy defending his frontiers in Asia Minor, the arrival of the Arabs under the command of Amr ibn al-As in A.D. 642–643 must have seemed little short of a liberation to the surviving inhabitants of the ancient Carthaginian Emporia. But of the three cities only one was to survive: this was Oea, which became the headquarters of the new occupying forces. By the end of the 7th century A.D., these forces had well and truly taken over Africa, including Carthage. Sabratha and Lepcis continued purely as Arab strongholds until the 9th century A.D., when they were engulfed by sand. Little but the memory of them remained until the day the Italian archaeologists' pick axes struck the ground at the beginning of the 20th century.

Lepcis, temple portico at the rear of the theater. In the foreground is an inscribed frieze that once ran along the façade of the Temple of the Augustan Deities. Built onto the temple was a huge, four-sided tetrapylon in honor of the Severan family. Behind the columns on the left is a re-erected panel with marble decoration from the back wall of the temple.

symbolizing the great Carthaginian goddess,"[12] then Tanit seems to be the undisputed (if not exclusive) mistress of *tophets* in both Oea and Sabratha. The pottery that was found with the stelae in Sabratha indicate that *tophet molchomor*, or substitute sacrifices, took place – in other words in the place of children, small animals were sacrificed, often newly born Saharan pigmy goats. This practice continued right through to the coming of the Roman empire.

Although it has been possible to refer some of the symbolic figures found on stelae in the Oea and Sabratha *tophets* not to Tanit but to her companion deity, Ba'al Hammon, nevertheless until very recently we had no direct evidence of the cult of Ba'al Hammon existing in Tripolitania. In April 1973, however, work was proceeding on an area rich in imperial-age structures just south of Sabratha, and a marble wash basin was found bearing a bilingual inscription in Latin and Punic: Ba'al Hammon's name appears to have been translated in the Latin text as "Saturn."

This new inscription from Sabratha provides direct evidence that the cult of the two Hammons – one from Carthage and the other of Egyptian-Libyan origin – existed simultaneously in Roman Tripolitania, albeit restricted to a social class mainly composed of Libyans under Carthaginian influence.

As has so rightly been pointed out, "in the religious history of Tripolitania, its geographical position must have played an important role, given its situation between the territory of Carthage, from which came the cult of Ba'al Hammon (who became Saturn in Roman times), and the Cyrenaican-Egyptian region, from where – from times that far pre-dated Carthaginian settlements – the cult of Ammon had spread (later to become Zeus-Jupiter Ammon in Greek and Roman culture)."[13]

On the other hand, it was from the Egyptian world that the Carthaginians of Tripolitania seem also to have borrowed the cult of Bes. The image of Bes as an inflexible god of fate, who is able to tame lions, can still be seen on the great frieze that decorated the façade of Mausoleum B in Sabratha.

Similarly, there is no doubt that Alexandria was the source of Serapis and Isis, divinities to whom large temples were built in both Lepcis and Sabratha; their cult came in through the Tripolitanian ports during the Hellenistic age. Indeed it is obvious that this is what occurred because, like the old Phoenician god Melkart, both Isis on her own and Isis and Serapis together offered protection to *naviculuraii*, navigators and seamen.

To sum up the cults found in Tripolitanian cities we can go along with P. A. Février,[14] who remarked that the "supremely astute move on the part of Roman imperialism" was not to impose its own institutions, but rather to offer a way of life to which people could aspire. Depending on the many different cultural, economic, and social backgrounds and classes, and even then

Imperial Administration

The proconsul and his legates

As we have room here only to outline the imperial administration in Roman Africa, we will deal with just the major posts.

All judicial, military, administrative, and financial powers of the senatorial province of Africa were initially concentrated in the hands of the proconsul. He resided in Carthage and was paid a very attractive annual salary; indeed, many considered it princely (250,000 *denarii*, in other words a million *sestertii* according to a report by the historian Dion Cassius referring to A.D. 217).

After the legate for the III Legion had been put in place, by Caligula's day the proconsul had virtually lost all military power. His authority was also limited with regard to financial administration: this came about during the 1st century A.D. as a consequence of the ever-growing importance of the financial procurator for Africa. Then, from the end of the 2nd century A.D., the emperor also nominated *curatores rei publicae*, whose powers replaced those of the proconsul with regard to the administration of individual cities in the province. Throughout all this, moreover, the length of time that any one proconsul remained in office was always short, usually just a year and very rarely anything over three.

The one thing that the proconsul did retain exclusively was judicial power. This persisted even after Diocletian pushed through his new order, which left the proconsul in charge of only a tiny part of the province of Africa. Similarly he held on to it even after Constantine's laws gave the final judgment in appeal cases to praetorian prefects only.

Evidence abounds of proconsuls interfering directly and indirectly in the affairs of the Tripolitanian cities; here I will mention only one example. In 1977 archaeologists made a discovery relating to the route of the ancient coast road between Sabratha and Oea: they found a milestone a quarter of a mile from Sabratha, undoubtedly the oldest milestone yet found in Tripolitania. The inscription engraved on it tells us that the road – following a natural route which had been widened and properly built – had been constructed over an earlier path by the legion on the orders of A. Caecina Severus, *suffectus* consul in 1 B.C.: Caecina Severus served as proconsul between about A.D. 8–9 and 12–13.

Aside from providing evidence of a new proconsul in Africa, this important inscription also proves that there was direct interference in the very territory of the "free and immune" Tripolitanian cities aimed at putting through an arterial road of primary strategic, and of course commercial, importance. Then again, we have a dedication from Lepcis which provides us with the latest mention – about the year A.D. 294 – of a proconsul in Tripolitania. By that date Tripolitania had already been a separate province for a number of years.

Among the literary evidence, the best-known passage comes from the *Apologia* of Apuleius, in which he defends himself against the charge of practicing magic, a work that mentions the judicial assizes held in the basilica at Sabratha. This refers to the annual tour that every provincial governor carried out specifically for the administration of justice. The one Apuleius describes was held by the proconsul Claudius Maximus in around A.D. 8: this was when the famous orator used his skills to save both his honor and indeed his life (see Appendix).

The strength of civic institutions in Africa was also apparent with respect to the proconsul. Though the provincial assembly had no control over the proconsul when he was in power, when he left office they could vote to honor him or not. Moreover, if they felt he had

Above: The market in Lepcis. Perimeter wall arcades facing toward the Via Trionfale. In front of these are marble stalls, elegantly carved.

Opposite: Lepcis, Severan complex. The entrances (in the center and on the left) lead to the "chamber of 13 columns" set under a wing of the perimeter portico of the forum and connecting the forum to the northwest end of the basilica. On the right is a shop doorway. The faced colonnade that runs along the back wall of the portico is mirrored on the external east wall of the basilica. For a general view of this area see pages 12–13: the arch shown here is in the left-hand corner.

Left: Lepcis, a street to the north of the theater. Arch stones from an arch commemorating the paving of the streets during the reign of Tiberius.

governed badly, they could accuse him of misconduct before the Senate in Rome.

In order to exercise their wide-ranging authority, African proconsuls, like those in other senatorial provinces, appointed legates. The legates' job was to represent the proconsul in everything except the final decisions in both civil litigation and penal cases.

Procuratores and curatores rei publicae

Although there is not a lot of evidence concerning the financial administration of ancient Tripolitania, what we have is significant.

The head of financial administration in Africa was the *procurator provinciae Africae*, an extremely important civil servant belonging to the equestrian order. It was his task to collect and send to Rome all taxes and tributes; he was also entrusted with looking after property "of the crown" and the emperor's personal property. However, from Hadrian's reign on, his functions with regard to indirect taxation shifted to an ad hoc procurator (the *procurator IIII publicarum Africae*). Then under Antoninus Pius the treasury was divided into the emperor's *patrimonium* and *res privata* (a complex division of the emperor's personal and imperial possessions that is still largely unclear). At the same time there was a growing tendency to decentralize services. All this led during the course of the 2nd century A.D. to the creation of an ever-greater number of specific imperial procurators.

So it was that different procurators were entrusted with the administration of property belonging to the imperial domains as well as the private estates of the emperor himself. In Africa, both categories were vast; as far as Tripolitania was concerned, however, they nearly all fell into the latter.

On the other hand, it has been shown that the Julio-Claudian dynasty already owned property in Oean territory, and even in the 2nd century A.D. the imperial house still owned property there. But it should be said that up to the time of the Severan dynasty, imperial property in Tripolitania remained far less important than elsewhere in Africa.

The situation changed when the Severans came to the throne. After this the private property of the emperors in the area became so extensive that they needed to set up a special office, which was probably based in Lepcis.

We also have a record of a procurator whose job it was to buy oil in Tripolitania and whose epitaph can be found in the Roman catacombs at Pretestato.

Without dwelling on the numerous lower grade civil servants who worked in the three cities, it is worthwhile noting how, through the records kept by procurators and *curatores* during the first 30 years of the 3rd century A.D., we can see the emergence within the imperial administration of a unifying regional concept. This gradually worked its way into the common assumptions of the ruling classes of Gightis, Sabratha, Oea, and Lepcis. So when Diocletian reshaped them into a province, it must have seemed the natural thing to do, both reinforcing existing physical boundaries and also promoting to the rank of government a regional administration that had been tested over time.

For Lepcis, which had always been the most important city in the region, the promotion to capital of the new Diocletian province was a natural step. It boasted long-standing loyalty to Rome and the growth of both its economy and its population had been quite exceptional. This was underpinned by a cleverly planned expansion of the town itself, which had started during its earliest days but was brilliantly accelerated during the Severan age. Moreover Lepcis possessed grandiose and splendid monuments. All of these elements meant that from Carthaginian times right up to the arrival of the Vandals, in the whole of Carthaginian-Roman Africa, Lepcis ranked second only to Carthage, so long as that city stood.

Above: Sabratha, House of Liber Pater. A mosaic lion's head in a paving medallion.

Opposite: Lepcis, the Nile Villa, along the shore between the port and the circus. A mosaic panel from corridor paving, showing scenes from a lion hunt (4th century AD).

LEPCIS

by Ginette Di Vita-Evrard

Introduction

Why this emptiness after joy?
Why this ending after glory?
Why this nothingness where once was a city?
Who will answer? Only the wind
Which steals the chantings of priests
And scatters the souls once gathered.
Sidi Mahrez

This medieval poet's lamentation for Carthage, the Phoenicians' western metropolis and the great Roman capital of Africa, could equally well apply to Lepcis. Today the sight that greets us is a place ruled only by the winds. Very few Roman remains from the western fringes of the empire are so forcefully able to conjure up not only an entire city, but also the very life of that city. Not many can convey to us today the idea of a place in which crowds of people lived, went about their business, enjoyed themselves. Not many give the sense of such a vast, unending place which, though not built of reinforced concrete, still banished the countryside, the green of nature, and gold of cultivated fields to the far distance, where the unchanging palm trees grow.

Normally the superimposition of the modern world on ancient sites creates such disparities that to some extent groups of ancient walls become an attraction appreciated only by the more sophisticated tourist. In Lepcis, the total absence of modernity immediately conjures up an extraordinarily powerful illusion of the past and plunges both the casual passerby and the specialist alike into the reality of a city that seems to live again. All you have to do is to take a stroll down the whole, sand-free length of a street that runs from the oasis toward the sea, which adds its own spindrift fringe to the heaps of toppled blocks. Italian archaeologists baptized this long, wide street the Via Trionfale, the

Triumphal Way. At the time it was the only road yet excavated with arcades down either side. Other streets intersected it at regular intervals, interrupting the rows of imposing, directly accessible public buildings. These alternated with ordinary houses, which can be glimpsed beneath embankments covered in broom and witchtongue. Every now and then you can see pavements, fountains, and carved "good luck" talismans. All this is set against a background of far larger monuments with high walls where an occasional decorated arch or column is still standing. Lepcis speaks to us immediately of a large city that was both complete and well organized. But this hidden history does not conflict with its weathered stones and its blossoming vegetation, whose effects change the appearance of the ruined city from month to month. It is still a place that engenders romantic reveries in passersby who are sensitive to what has come to be known as the poetry of ruins.

Certainly, huge tracts of the city are still buried beneath the oasis sand; but nothing of vital importance is missing. We now have a complete list of the monuments you would expect to find in an urban area run on municipal lines. A few remains from mausoleums, plus the abundant funeral material on display in the museum there, tells us about the world of the dead. We can accept that future finds might paint a more subtle and varied picture; but it will not be a completely different one. When most tourists leave the site, their heads reeling with facts provided by their guide, they feel they have acquired cultural souvenirs bearing the hallmark of certainty. Nonetheless, supposition and controversy, differing interpretations, and enigmas of detail will continue to feed those with a keener curiosity; archaeologists and historians of the future will continue their learned musings. No one will blame us, therefore, if we allow some of these doubts to surface

Above: Marble medallion from arcades in the Severan Forum. The head of Medusa.

Opposite: Colonnade to the rear of the theater stage (southeast end). The inscription on the flat planes of the architrave commemorates the construction of the theater. At the foot of the fluted columns stand the shafts of smaller columns from the two higher orders, which have not been put back into position. The absence of the rear stage wall, which archaeologists have not rebuilt, allows us to see the gray granite columns, topped by white marble Corinthian capitals, that belong to the large portico behind the theater (see page 34).

THREE COLUMNS BY THE SEA

Between 1686 and 1708 Claude Le Maire twice
served as French Consul to the Ottoman Regency in
Tripoli. Drawing his inspiration from recent, albeit
sporadic, precedents, he set up a thriving business in
ancient marble from Lepcis, which was reused in
monuments then under construction in France. In this
he had connivance from the "commander of the
Moors in the Lepida area."
Contemporary navy documents in the French National
Archive tell us all about how the marble was extracted,
how the columns were loaded and shipped, and how
many there were, divided into category, color, size,
and unit price.
At the time, Lepcis was still buried under a mantle of
sand several meters thick. The few structures that
protruded here and there signaled the presence of
large monuments – in other words, potential deposits.
Claude Le Maire himself left a single memo detailing
the reasons why three columns of "green and white
undulated marble," as cipolin was then called, were
abandoned on the seashore. The columns came from
the Great Baths (but were mistaken for a triumphal
arch) where they had already found another seven
which were "27 feet long, intact and complete with
their pedestals." He wrote, "I have been working for
over five months* to free the three huge columns from
the sand ... I cannot ship them as I do not have a
barge strong enough to carry them on board the
King's store ship."
Dozens of smaller columns were shipped, probably
taken from the Severan Forum and the Via Colonnata.
There were either reused intact or, more often, split
into slabs as happened at Versailles. A few years
later, some more columns from Lepcis were shipped
to London, and to Windsor Great Park.

G.D.V.-E.

*Another version emphasizes not how long it took, but how
dangerous it was: "Three long months under canvas during the
sweltering heat of summer and exposed to Arab raids."

*Cipolin columns from the frigidarium in
Hadrian's Baths, buried for three centuries
to the north of the old forum. The street
in the foreground follows a route that
runs along the shoreline (see map on
page 51, top). In the distance is the modern
town of Homs.*

complex to the smallest detail, was influenced by what was happening in the city of cities, the center of power.

We can easily imagine how from 30–20 B.C., just after the civil wars, two parties emerged in Lepcis: one was pro-Roman and possessed great foresight; the other was a more traditionalist party. Lepcis' great fortune was to fall into the hands of the former, a small and extremely rich aristocratic land-owning and merchant class. These people traveled to Rome and were well informed about new political, ideological, architectural, and cultural trends. At the local level, they were firmly committed to the push for modernity, but at the same time were wise enough not to break with the cultural, religious, and linguistic traditions of their long heritage. One man sums up all these qualities: Annobal Tapapius Rufus, son of Himilcho. The literary tradition of Rome has made us more familiar with the Latin form of his name, Hannibal. His full name is a clear indication of his position in society. He was an immensely rich Lepcitian who had held the highest position in the city's magistrature, that of *suffect* (priest). He had also held local or new priestly offices as well being an imperial *flamen* (priest). Annobal Rufus had been to Augustan Rome, and had seen its monuments and building projects. He was an ambitious man who was well aware of the political impact "major works" had on people's minds – of the power exercised by the symbolic images and inscriptions on the façades of great monuments. He learned Augustus' lesson in publicity and propaganda, and used it both for the common good and for his own advantage, adapting these new communication values to the situation in Lepcis, where he played the role Augustus played in the Roman empire.

His first project was the market; the dedicatory inscription dates its completion to the year 8 B.C. The marble facing, the reworked entrances and their adjoining spaces to the east cannot disguise the originality of the layout. The way it was built and the site selected, for the reasons explained above, mark Lepcis out for the specialized and sophisticated methods of town planning it used in its public spaces. The forum was above all the place of official religion; it could also accommodate religion's close relatives: politics, trade, law, and culture. But the forum was no longer big enough to accommodate a market, especially not a food market. First uncovered in the 1930s, and partly rebuilt just after World War II, the market remains one of the most evocative buildings in the city. Of its type, it is the most elegant in the whole of the Roman world. The huge space is enclosed by porticoes, inherited from Hellenistic agoras. Inside, in the shade of the porticoes, light partitions divided up the shops; or perhaps there were just rows of counters, ancestors of the fine marble tables with animal feet that were to come later. The architect of Lepcis market drew his inspiration from an existing motif: that of a circular structure enclosed in a rectangular one. But he created a variant on this that has remained unique. He dared to have two and not the usual one circular structure (*tholos*) and then to give them huge dimensions: they are almost 20 meters (65 feet) in diameter. He arranged a regular row of market benches under the arcades of the cylindrical core of one of these two circular constructions: its counterpart housed a fountain, which was essential to work in the market. Another row of counters was housed between the colonnades of the structures' octagonal perimeters, thus giving them a functional, rather than a purely decorative, appearance. Archaeologically speaking, very little is known of markets of this era, and so it is unwise to try to identify a model for Lepcis market. Nevertheless, documentary sources from the 1st century B.C. lead us to believe that there was a *tholos* like this in the *macellum* (meat market) in Rome.

Because of the way the land lies, this huge rectangular space enclosed by high walls was mounted on a terrace which totally dominated the Via Trionfale. Nevertheless, its long wall, pierced by tall arcades, does not open onto the main street nor onto much of the street that runs along its east side. Access, marked by a single column, is from a corner flight of steps at the point where two streets intersect. These two sides of the vast enclosure house small, outward-facing shops which disguise the lack of alignment and the irregularities in the level of the ground. The main entrance halfway along the west side originally had two arched doorways. One of these has not been reworked and its keystone still bears the *caduceus*, the staff of Mercury, the god of commerce; the *caduceus* was much prized in both Punic and Augustan symbolism. The high sandstone walls were stuccoed and painted both inside and out. At the point where the main entrance was located, the wall opened onto a hollow space, created by

Above: This tablet, found in the market, shows the official length measures used during the 1st century A.D.: the Punic cubit, the Alexandrine cubit, and the Roman foot as well as their divisions. At the site itself, a plaster cast replaces the original, which is now displayed in the Lepcis Museum.

Opposite: The market in Lepcis. The northwest tholos seen from the west through the axes of the two doors. Clearly visible are the holes for the roof beams of the surrounding octagonal portico (the portico columns can be seen through the archway of the furthest door and in the foreground).

Below: Lepcis, inner portico of the market. Marble bases for the market stalls (2nd century A.D.). In the background, to the left, an isolated column belonging to the southeast entrance.

نسخة لوحدات
قياس طولية
A COPY FOR UNITS
LENGTH MEASURES

Preceding pages: The market in Lepcis. The northwest tholos viewed from the south. Between the columns of the portico, stone market stalls stand on animal bases. These were gifts from the aediles whose names can be read on the left: Ti(berius) C(laudius) Amicus, M(arcus) Heliodorius Apollonides.

Opposite: The market in Lepcis. The northwest tholos seen from the northwest. In the foreground, the reerected section of the octagonal portico. Between the corner pillar, to the left, and the column stands a market stall which was later used as the coping of a well, hence the rope marks.

Right: The market in Lepcis, general view seen from the northeast. All that remains of the southeast tholos on the left is its octagonal portico.

the way the axes of the streets met. This became a piazza where people met, waited for each other, talked: in short the ideal place for communication. Annobal chose this outer wall to bear an inscription that could not be missed by anyone. The earliest Latin monumental text that we have in Lepcis, it consists of a two-line, centered banner that unfurls between the two doorways and is some 25 meters (82 feet) long and set about four meters (13 feet) above the door arches. The name of Augustus, followed by that of the governor of the province of Africa, precedes the mention of the *suffecti* and priests in a very early cult dedicated to the deified emperor. There then follows the name of the donor, together with the titles of the offices he holds, and an explicit mention of his generosity. For the benefit of his less well-educated fellow citizens, Annobal's text is repeated in Neo-Punic on the curved limestone blocks that crown the inner ring of the

south *tholos*. A few decades later, at the end of Tiberius' reign, the only proconsul whom we know interfered with the running of the city (but even this was a trade-off for the city regaining agricultural land) paid for the paving of the areas where people walked; he commemorated his public works by simple arches across the streets – one even leant against the market – and dedicated them to Tiberius. At this time the piazza was given a double openwork portico in the Hellenistic style; despite later bastardized rebuilding work, column bases still show where this originally stood. Like any self-respecting market, the one in Lepcis had its official weights and measures, not just for capacity and weight, but also for length. All the indications are that the produce market supplied a wide range of delicious foodstuffs for the everyday tables of the rich or for special occasions of the less well-off. It probably also sold other products, such as fabrics.

No sooner had Annobal Rufus inaugurated the market than he started work on a second and far more imposing building project, a theater. The decision-makers of Lepcis allocated this a slightly hilly plot, used earlier, between the 5th and 3rd centuries B.C., as a cemetery. After Sabratha, this theater is the second largest of its kind surviving in Africa. It was, however, the earliest in date – even in Rome the first stone-built theater had been constructed only 50 years before.

The lower part of the semicircular seating tiers was carved directly out of the rock. There were two main access galleries running down toward the orchestra. At the top, the tiers of seating rested on an artificial embankment that was reinforced on the inside. The whole of the seating area was contained by a plain semicircular wall faced in pink sandstone, a wall so big it now completely dominates the surrounding ruins. This wall is given a vertical rhythm by pilasters, and is cut horizontally by a simple cornice running round the lower

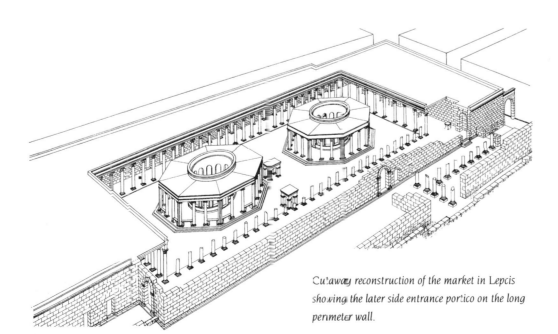

Cutaway reconstruction of the market in Lepcis showing the later side entrance portico on the long perimeter wall.

Preceding pages: The market in Lepcis.
The northwest tholos viewed through the
columns of the west wing of the courtyard
portico. These are in gray granite from
Asia Minor and probably date from the

benches for the decurions in the *cella*. The purpose of the building is also obvious from the honorifics – some of which date from after the middle of the second century – carved on *antae* or on statue plinths.

The history of the precolonial forum ends with a building dating from Trajan's reign. The original layout of the building is little understood, but it formed a pair with the Temple of Cybele on the other side, at the beginning of the Via Trionfale. Much later on this building was turned into a church. Its molded base, which gives an indication of the date in which building first began, was obviously fashioned from blocks of that time. It may have been the building known as the *basilica Ulpia*, probably from Trajan's name (Marcus Ulpius Traianus), unless Ulpius was also the name of the local notable who built it. This basilica was mentioned in an inscription from the Tetrarchy period, but so far archaeologists have failed to locate it.

Port, amphitheater, and commemorative monuments

We can now leave the forum and travel back in time. Two large building complexes, both dating from before the Flavian era, and now in very different states of preservation, also belong to the city of stone.

The modern visitor would never notice the first one, even though it was of major importance. This was the port on the promontory, with the wadi to one side and facing the sea to the north. The town was originally built on the promontory (later joined to the small islands) but it had no natural port. To compensate, engineering work was begun on the northeast and east shores of the promontory. In particular, the western part of the wide wadi bed (which filled with water only during torrential rain) appears to have been dug out and encased in powerful concrete masonry more than 10 meters (33 feet) thick for a stretch of at least 150 meters (490 feet). An inscription from Nero's reign, describing a three-way portico built partly on private, partly on public land, provided a clue as to the appearance of the quays on the promontory. Furthermore, drilling work had suggested the existence of a port-canal, which was confirmed by floods in the 1980s. The floodwaters scooped out the ground beneath road level at the far end of the Severan Via Colonnata, which covered the port-canal, sweeping its structure bare; experts are still studying the detail of its complex layout. Shade from a portico running along the canal, at least on the town side, added the finishing touch to the work on this early port. It is quite probable that in this period the first dam was built to control the waters of the wadi upstream of the site and thus ensure that the port was protected.

Preceding pages: The amphitheater in Lepcis. A view from inside. The terracing of the doors marks the different horizontal sectors in the cavea. In the middle of the arena, the rows of blocks trace the underground service areas, which are now filled with sand. At regular intervals in the top of the podium wall there are holes that housed posts holding a vast canvas sunscreen over the spectators. The three rows beneath this, especially those on the south side, which enjoyed the cooling sea breeze, were reserved for VIPs. Amid these seats was the box of honor (center, bottom), which had its own private entrance. The seating tiers have been painstakingly restored, though they are still missing on the north side, toward the circus and the sea.

Opposite: Hunting Baths in Lepcis. This large fresco decorating the west wall of the frigidarium depicts a leopard hunt (venatio) performed in the amphitheater. Evocative names were often given to both hunters and animals.

This page, top and bottom (detail): A section from the gladiator frieze of a famous mosaic at Dar Buc Ammera (Zliten). Top, from left to right: musicians; a duel between Samnite gladiators halted by a lanista or trainer; a retiarius (net fighter) and his opponent; and a duel between secutores (gladiators who wield axes).

life. These were carefully maintained, repaired, and renovated by local worthies or by the community at large. In this manner, the Augustan gateways to the market were replaced, and Annobal's beautiful inscription obliterated in the process. Most importantly, the south *tholos* of the market was rebuilt in a beautiful silvery-gray limestone that becomes golden as weathering gives it a patina. The local notables always knew how to be generous: one of them honored Cybele with a temple; in Domitian's time, another built a temple on the east bank of the wadi. But the outstanding personality on the Lepcitian scene under the last of the Flavian emperors was the very image of the vain locally elected man so vividly described in Horace's satires: this was Tiberius Claudius Sestius. He used the stones of Lepcis to flaunt his career, his titles, and the honors he had been awarded thanks to the "merits" of his ancestors – and, of course, his own. These honors even included permission, granted in perpetuity, to wear ceremonial dress (an indication of rank usually reserved for solemnities only) every day of the year. In A.D. 92 he paid to have the tiers of seating in the theater orchestra improved; he also had a limestone altar placed in the middle of the tiers and a stone parapet built to separate dignitaries from the rest of the audience. It was upon this parapet that his indiscreet elegy was carved. Translated rather less visibly into Neo-Punic for those citizens who did not speak Latin, this was placed on one side of the altar dedicated to an Augustan divinity, Liber Pater, or Apollo. It cannot be ruled out that Tiberius Claudius Sestius might also have been connected to the temple dedicated two years later to the deified Domitian, who was still alive, and also to his father and brother, who had also been deified. This was an imperial sanctuary, built to the west of the forum, whose porticoed terrace dominated the quayside in the port. Yet again, the idea of a temple with twin deities seems to have come from the capital of the empire. Here, this sanctuary, probably built by a rich local worthy about A.D. 100, with its courtyard and porticoes overlooking the sea, could well have been inspired by a famous monument of Flavian Rome. The civic community commemorated their ascent in legal status, achieved through awards dispensed by successive emperors, with exemplary pomp and displays of loyalty, and they carved their gratitude to the emperors in stone. Vespasian made them a *municipium* under Roman law,

and in A.D. 77–78 Lepcis demonstrated its loyalty by constructing a new building to commemorate its status – this building has not been found, though a stone panel, engraved on both sides, has been preserved. This has traditionally been attributed to an arch some 50 cm (20 inches) thick, but there now seems little doubt that it must have come from the lintel of a doorway in an outer wall. This, and a carved frieze more than 10 meters (33 feet) long, is all that we have of the building. In A.D. 110, Trajan established Lepcis as an honorary Roman colony: in return they honored him with the first *quadrifrons* (four-way) arch in Lepcis. This stands at a main crossroads close to the *chalcidicum* and the market, where the Via Trionfale joins. The arch, which disguises a slight bend in the road, was constructed from the finest limestone veins from Ras el-Hamman. There were inscriptions on two faces of the frieze and attic, above the groups of statues that must once have been on the arch. The inscriptions explain why, and in what circumstances, the arch was erected. At least in Africa, it was

Lepcis which introduced the innovation of making an arch a monument for commemorating and expressing gratitude for the attainment of a higher legal status. Symbolically, this jewel of travertine limestone brings to a close the period in which marble was not used, even in the most refined buildings.

Hadrian's Baths, Lepcis: the pool in the
center of the tepidarium. The steps are still
clad in marble. The columns are of a gray
marble that probably came from Algeria
(Cape Garde).

Water and Marble
The 2nd century A.D.

From the start of Hadrian's reign two circumstances
combined to transform both the city's way of life and the
appearance of its buildings.

One of the advantages of Lepcis' location was that it
had several freshwater springs, as well as plentiful rainwater, to fill up large storage cisterns. In fact, rainfall was
higher in Roman times than in later centuries, when the
immediate hinterland became a desert. We know from
excavations that even with these limited water supplies
there was at least one public baths, probably dating
from the second half of the 1st century. These baths were
not very big, taking up just one block of the city grid
quite close to the shore. A very scanty inscription from
around A.D. 101–102 refers to some work that could have
been these baths (or perhaps others).

The need for a water supply of better quality and reli-
ability must have grown increasingly urgent as the city's
population increased rapidly and the city adopted a lifes-
style that copied the Roman model, where the baths
played an ever-greater role. True to sound local custom,
it was a member of the rich middle classes who resolved
the problem once and for all. Named Quintus Servilius
Candidus, he belonged to a family coming from the elite
of Lepcis; we can trace the history of this family, directly
and indirectly, until just after the middle of the 3rd
century A.D. As could be expected, the family's wealth
was mainly derived from landed property. In this connection, we have their oil amphora stamps dating from the
middle of the 2nd century A.D., a rarity, and also from the
3rd century; we also have the tomb of Quintus Servilius
Candidus' estate manager, which was found recently. In
the middle of the 2nd century A.D. the Servilii family
commissioned a villa, which is one of the nearest along
the coast from the town; it is the only villa there whose
owners are identifiable from specially stamped bricks. At
the end of the 2nd century A.D. a local worthy chose a
bride closely related to the family; in the 3rd century A.D.,
if not earlier, the family became members of the senate
and entered the service of empire. This sums up their
social position; and it would be surprising if they had not
already acquired Roman citizenship under Claudius, just
like the ancestors of Tiberius Claudius Sestius. At his
own expense, Quintus Servilius Candidus set about
finding, extracting, pumping, and supplying year-round
water for Lepcis, perhaps with imperial authorization.
On some small, inscribed plinths found in the theater,
Quintus Servilius Candidus credits Emperor Hadrian
with the merit of guaranteeing "the eternity of water." It
seems very likely that the aqueduct was none other than

Opposite: Lepcis, Hadrian's Baths. In the foreground is the large east-end changing room, opening onto the swimming pool (to the right). In the background, the frigidarium. The marble cladding hides the structure of the wall, which is composed of hewn stone and rubble, a widespread construction technique in Africa which archaeologists call opus africanum.

Right: Lepcis, Hadrian's Baths. The large west-end pool of the frigidarium, seen from the east (the arcades at the far end belong to the wide corridor that encircled the "cold block." Between the columns around the pool stood statues of gods, their images reflected in the water. These statues were often 2nd century A.D. *copies of Greek originals. Most were still in place when the site was excavated, and are now in Tripoli Museum.*

The pedestrian sidewalk still carried on toward the northeast, following a detour that took it clear of the new building.

The interior layout of the baths was borrowed from what was known as the imperial type. In Rome, this is illustrated by the Baths of Nero, the Baths of Titus and above all, immediately prior to this date, the Baths of Trajan. The hallmark of imperial baths was total symmetry, even of the secondary or peripheral rooms, in relation to a main axis. In Lepcis the axis ran from north to south. There was always a porticoed courtyard surrounding a large open-air swimming pool, *frigidarium* (a cold room), *tepidarium* (a warm room), and *caldaria* (hot rooms) The hot rooms were especially spacious and their axis was perpendicular to the main axis. To the north, east, and west there were thermal rooms and plenty of large rooms for various purposes: dressing rooms, exercise rooms, and indoor areas where people could stroll or meet each other. All of this, as we would expect, made baths the center of the city's social and cultural life, an aspect facilitated by the excellent pedestrian traffic system operating in the baths. Corridors led off two side doors, doubling the number of people who could go through the big swimming pool courtyard, and extended into small side areas that an inscription describes as *crypta*. These were, in fact, galleries about four meters (13 feet) wide, looping into a second aisle at either end of the long sides of the building, which stretched for an astonishing 74 meters (245 feet). The galleries surrounded the oblong rectangular block of the *frigidarium* with its side swimming pools and isolated it from the hot zone. The use of galleries is a variant not seen in other baths and clearly indicates the originality the architects of Lepcis could display when employing a standard plan. The galleries allowed a totally different use to be made of the various rooms and, as they were closed to the outside, they also provided places where people could walk in what must have been much-appreciated freshness.

Throughout the Roman world baths were always extremely popular, and this must have been particularly true in Lepcis because of its climate. Nonetheless, the baths were also a place of privilege where the local gentry could display their wealth: they were anxious to maintain the baths properly, to improve and embellish them, and at the same time to leave behind in the building both their names and sculpted portraits. Marble facing was an integral part of the original building concept, as we can see from the dated quarry marks on the back of the slabs. At first, however, the use

The greater part of the medallions show Gorgon heads which, like Minerva's shield, were a symbol of the Roman goddess Victory and were taken from a well-known repertory which had been associated for centuries with the ornamental programs in imperial forums and temples. A few medallions show heads of sea creatures and have been given different interpretations: are they Nereids (sea nymphs), or the sea monster Scylla? Or perhaps the Syrian mother goddess Atargatis, which would have been a clear reference to the divine powers of the empress, Julia Domna, so often associated with imperial Victory? This has yet to be determined.

The old forum was not abandoned, deserted, or neglected; nevertheless, the Severan Forum became the new official political center. It was here that henceforward people would make their frequent homages to emperors, governors, and important people of the city. This practice has left us with a wonderful series of inscribed plinths and a few rare statues that are more or less intact; both were frequently reused for the same purpose over the decades that followed.

Because the inscription we have is too meager, it is not clear to which divinity the temple in the Severan Forum was dedicated; perhaps it was Augustan Concorde.

All the evidence, nevertheless, points to the fact that in one way or the other it was dedicated to the cult of the imperial dynasty. Its relatively modest size was made up for by the height of the podium and the monumentality of the staircase, which had two griffins at its base. Then there was the conspicuous wealth of its Egyptian granite colonnade, triple at the front, mounted on a marble dais. The colonnade and, to a lesser extent, the façade columns, were carved with a finely crafted battle scene between giants and gods, the Gigantomachia: giants whose feet are serpents are set against a coalition of gods in which the Eastern divinities mingle with the inhabitants of Olympus.

There has been a whole series of studies dedicated to the provenances of the marbles and of the specialist team of masons and sculptors who worked on this project, some of whom left their names, in Greek, on the marble components. Major disagreements aside, scholars do not even agree on the role played in the development of Lepcis by the major Greek cities in Asia Minor, an involvement already touched on in connection with the architectural and decorative choices made for Lepcis' Roman forum. Some aspects of this involvement are direct, many others are indirect; but it is clear that by

Left: Lepcis. Southeast corner of the Severan Forum. In the background is the basilica wall, and on the far right the brick-and-stone wall that separates the forum from the Via Colonnata. In front of the central medallion, which was a corner piece, is the base of the corner pillar of the portico's second order.

Above: Lepcis. The entrance exedra of the Severan Basilica viewed from the forum. In the foreground, to the right, is a column base stood on end, showing the shaft fastening device (a central channel for metal rods).

Following pages: Lepcis. Severan Forum. The back wall of the portico set against the basilica. In front of the row of richly framed shop doorways stand capitals and pieces of entablature from the attached columns, whose pedestals all survive.

SABRATHA

by Antonino Di Vita

From Seasonal Trading Post to Punic City

For many years the date in which the city was established has been controversial; so too is the date of the early staging post built up around a small natural harbor. We do, however, have strong evidence from a series of soundings the British School of Rome took in 1948, 1949, and 1951 beneath the oldest part of town, between the forum and the sea. The soundings also covered the forum itself, the Temple of Liber Pater and the Antonine Temple, and continued down the *insula* that runs from north to south behind these buildings.

Beneath stone structures dating at the earliest from the 4th century B.C. in the *insulae* closest to the sea – that

is to say in the areas the archaeologists designated as *regio* II, 5, 6, 7[1] – virgin ground yielded post holes in beaten earth, and carbon-rich soil strata separated by layers of sand brought in on the wind. J. B. Ward-Perkins and K. Kenyon, who organized this dig, rightly deduced that the actual settlement had been preceded by a seasonal trading post used year after year. Some rare Attic fragments allow us to put a date on this seasonal settlement of around the last quarter of the 5th century B.C. Also discovered were a few stretches of wall that may have been a line of defense for the earliest permanent settlement: 2.5 meters (8 feet) wide, they are sited

Left: Sabratha. View of the Baths, seen from the north. In the background, silhouetted against the skyline, is the theater.

Opposite: Sabratha theater. Middle section of the stage wall, seen from an inner gallery.

square or nearly square and measure between 20 and 25 meters (65.5 and 98.4 feet) across. Many people have noted their similarity to the square blocks of housing at Timgad, a town built by soldiers of the III *legio* in 100 B.C. in the depths of Algeria. The comparison is relevant, and it does seem highly probable that the layout used for the new urban development was that used by Roman colonists.

The first *insula* encountered along the coast road contained a temple which repeated the layout of the temple dedicated to an "unknown divinity." Here the temple was dedicated to Hercules, the Roman manifestation of the ancient and much-worshipped Phoenician-Punic god Melkart. The second *insula* housed baths (now known as the Theater Baths), which spread southward over the adjacent block.

The theater was not built until the reign of Commodus – according to some scholars later still, under Septimus Severus. Nevertheless, it seems likely that it formed part of the same urban development project. This theater is now quite spectacular, for the archaeologist who excavated it, Giacomo Guidi, and his successor Giacomo Caputo, managed to rebuild the whole of the impressive stage building, which had been completely flattened by the earthquake. This now makes it one of the most enjoyable theaters in the Roman world. The alignment of the theater and its *porticus post-scaenam*, the portico behind the stage, is slightly offset compared to that of the surrounding *insulae*. This must have been determined, I believe, by problems to do with the free circulation of traffic between the theater and the neighboring quarries, especially since one of the main routes from town toward the interior ran directly through them.

If indeed the theater does date from around A.D. 190, this means that there are no monuments in Sabratha from the Severan age except the large base of a *quadriga* dedicated to Septimus Severus in A.D. 202 and erected at the expense of an unknown Sabrathan. This occupies the open space at the entrance to the new quarters where the *platea* terminates as it swings south of *regiones* VI and V.

Sabratha: View of columns standing on the tall podium of the Temple of Liber Pater (in the center); gray granite Mysian columns of the south wing of the forum (left of center); and (far left) stylobate and cipolin columns belonging to the Byzantine basilica to the south of the forum. In the background, on the far right, a statue of Flavius Tullus (?) stands near one of the fountains that Tullus donated to the citizens of Sabratha.

CYRENAICA

by Lidiano Bacchielli

and Claudio Parisi Presicce
and Serenella Ensolli

followed the systematic plan of demolishing and replacing all the earlier buildings in the area (some of which dated back to the late 6th century B.C.), so that the orientation of the new quarter was quite different from that of the earlier one.

This new urban space took its character from the major building of the area, the Hellenistic Gymnasium, which stands to the east. The result was a grid of rectangular blocks, positioned at right angles along the major axis formed by the ridge of the hill. Within this grid are a number of mid-2nd century B.C. monuments, of which the most important is the Gymnasium itself, both in terms of its scale, its function, and its regal clientele.

The way in which the new blocks were carefully adapted to fit the line of the perimeter wall, which is especially obvious in the southern section of the east wall, suggests that the grid and the wall were defined at the same time, as part of a single overall plan. Over 5.5 kilometers (3.4 miles) long, the new wall encloses the full extent of the known city. It was designed to take full advantage of the terrain, following the edge of the plateau wherever possible, and making use of the contours of the hillside. The square defensive towers were concentrated in the flat sections.

It is more difficult to distinguish the different phases of the development of the other quarters of the city. Excavations have been concentrated on the areas immediately surrounding certain major monuments; outside these areas, we have to rely mainly upon aerial photographs. In the northern part of the hill, in what we might call the Olympeion quarter, the principal axis seems to have been defined by the Temple of Zeus. In the part of the site that is nearest to the central valley, the main axis, running east-west, is not perfectly straight, but is made up of various sections aligned according to the demands of the terrain. The subsidiary north-south axes run at right angles to these different sections of the main axis, and so the clusters of buildings that lie on the border between two different sections are of irregular shape. For these last two zones, the small amount of information that can be gleaned from aerial photographs suggests that they were only ever partially built.

Cyrene, Sanctuary of Apollo. Part of the Skyrotà, the "Sacred Way" that linked the square in front of the Temple of Apollo to the oracle's grotto.

There are four churches in Apollonia: one in the eastern part of the city, one in the center, one in the west, and a fortified church which stood outside the walls. The East Basilica has a transept and is divided into three naves by tall columns made of cipolin marble and crowned with capitals taken from earlier edifices. Traces remain of an altar and a ciborium dating from the 5th century A.D., when the mosaics of the apse were executed. The upper level of the mosaic in the transept depicting Noah, his ark and the animals, dates from the reign of Emperor Justinian, as does the baptistery, built to a trefoil plan, which stands on the site of an earlier square chapel.

Above: Apollonia. The theater: the cavea (auditorium) was partly cut into the rock.

Right: Apollonia. The Central Basilica, view from the apse looking west.

as elements that had already been made and were simply lying in the cellars of the *proconessus*, the marble store, awaiting their destination.

The Metropolitan Basilica stands in the west of the city. It is a massive structure, with three naves lined with pillars. Next to the apse there are two surviving rooms, one on a trefoil plan (with a well-preserved cupola), the other on a cruciform plan. In front of the naves is a narthex in the form of a portico with two arcades. It is flanked by two rooms, one of which houses the staircase leading to the upper floor, the other a narrow door leading outside. A second equally small door can be found in the wall of the northern nave. The tiny dimensions of these entrances and the great width of the walls suggest that this was a fortified church, like the one that had been built at Berenice to protect the inhabitants against nomadic incursions.

Preceding pages: Ptolemais. The Teuchira Gate in the city walls.

Above: Ptolemais. The Columned Palace.

Right: Ptolemais. The West Basilica.

APPENDIX

Apuleius' Apologia: The Wealth of Tripolitania in the Days of Antoninus Pius

by Antonino Di Vita

Apuleius, who liked to describe himself as "Platonic philosopher," was a famous rhetorician accused of using magic to entrap a rich widow, Pudentilla, the mother of his friend and former fellow-student Pontianus. The charge would have meant the death penalty had his brilliant defense plea to Proconsul Claudius Maximus not succeeded (about A.D. 157–158). The plea has survived: it is his famous *Pro se de magia*, better known as the *Apologia*.

Let's review the facts. Apuleius was in Sabratha for a few days attending to his wife's business, including a law suit to be heard by the proconsul. Claudius Maximus was, in fact, on his tour of the province and stopped in Sabratha to hear cases. Apuleius was in his lodgings at one of the city's inns sorting out his business when suddenly the brother of Pudentilla's first husband, an old man called Sicinius Aemilianus, had him arrested. He was brought before the proconsul on charges of casting spells on Aemilia Pudentilla, *mulier locupletissima* ("a very rich woman"), who had stubbornly remained a widow for 14 years but was now married to Apuleius.

Sicinius Aemilianus had acted on behalf of Pudentilla's youngest son, Sicinius Pudens, who, although only a youth, was already well on the road to ruin. He shirked his studies and shunned good company and had fallen in with a bad crowd, including gladiators (it is worth mentioning in passing that this is the sole evidence we have of an amphitheater in Oea during the reign of Antoninus Pius).

Not only was Sicinius Aemilianus a rogue but, according to Apuleius, he was also an ignorant brute. To help him with the legal action, he hired an army of lawyers headed by a Tannonius Pudens, a mediocre lawyer from Oea (or perhaps Sabratha). It was he who put together the lengthy and detailed case against

Apuleius, who was granted just over 24 hours to get his defense ready for the proconsul. The proconsul, surrounded by counselors, chancellors, and *nomenclatores*, held court in the basilica on the south side of the forum. The fascinated crowd was mainly made up of fairly uneducated provincials who were attracted in great numbers by the fact that Apuleius was an extremely well-known orator, and that Pudentilla had been a highly desirable widow.

Keeping one eye on the water running rapidly through an hourglass that measured the time allowed for his defense (the same amount of time was allotted to the prosecution), Apuleius improvised from his notes. Charge by charge, he used sheer weight of detail to refute the calumnies, confound his accuser, attack the ignorance of the lawyers, and unmask the witnesses. One of them, Junius Crassus from Oea, had been suborned by Sicinius Aemilianus and his abject accomplice Herennius Rufinus, whom Apuleius described as spending his life propping up bars, rolling drunk in broad daylight, and making a nuisance of himself at Sabratha's public baths.

The brilliant way Apuleius defended himself, the way he flattered Maximus, the patent untruth of the charge, together with the prosecuting team's lack of experience, meant that he was set free; as far as we can tell, he had been found not guilty on all counts. Thus it was that he lived to write up his defense speech and it is this document which, when stripped of all its rhetoric, erudite exhibitionism, and paradoxes, paints such a lively and vivid picture of provincial life. But that is not all. Two factors contained in the plea make it valuable to us.

Firstly, the sums of money involved were real and would have been difficult to falsify (and indeed some were documented) at a trial presided over by the highest authority in the province.

Secondly, we know the exact dates the sums relate to (the reign of Antoninus Pius). Because Roman currency was so stable, we can go as far as saying that the *Apologia* provides us with a financial yardstick, if not for all of proconsular Africa, at least for Tripolitania. And we can use this yardstick for the whole of the first and most of the second centuries of the empire.

Indeed, Apuleius would have weakened his defense had he interfered substantially with the figures. We must not forget that the trial (which after all was about money) was held in Sabratha and was about events that happened in Oea. The two places were so close that not only did people directly involved know the facts and the figures, but so did many of the observers in the crowd. Undoubtedly, Apuleius would have pushed everything as far as he possibly could without going so far as to jeopardize his credibility. He would have massaged the facts so long as this did not weaken his defense. The *Apologia* proves he was too intelligent, too cunning, and too much in control not to have calculated the counter-productive effect that an obviously "cooked" balance sheet from the marriage settlement might have had not just on the judge, the proconsul, but above all on the people of Sabratha, who, well informed and highly critical, exhibited a morbid fascination for it all.

Let's start with the main characters in this business. Apuleius married Pudentilla, a lady from Oea and a widow whom a lot of men had been after because of her money. But Apuleius himself did not exactly come from a penniless family, and of course did not fail to point this out in his defense speech. He was the son of a well-heeled citizen from Madaura who had risen through the ranks in the course of his municipal career, the *cursus honorum*, ending up as a *duumvir*. On his death, he left his two sons an inheritance

of two million *sestertii*, generally considered a substantial sum.

As for Pudentilla, everyone agreed that she was a rich woman. Her estate, valued at four million *sestertii*, included a mixture of town houses and high-yield farmland 160 kilometers (100 miles) away from Sabratha[1] which produced, among other things, large quantities of corn, barley, wine, and olive oil. The land was also used for grazing flocks of sheep, herds of cattle, and even horses. Pudentilla owned enough slaves on her land to be able to give 400 of them to her children without really noticing it.

Despite this extensive wealth, when she remarried Pudentilla paid a dowry of only 300,000 *sestertii*. This was a really small dowry for a woman from such a wealthy family. Just compare this to the daughter of Herennius Rufinus from Oea, a member of the team prosecuting Apuleius. When his daughter married, her father paid a dowry of 400,000 *sestertii*, a reasonable sum for a "middle-class" girl[2], but quite out of proportion to Herennius Rufinus' means.

Indeed, the picture Apuleius paints of Herennius Rufinus is of a ruined man who had only managed to put his daughter's dowry together by borrowing left, right, and center – a man from the best Oean society but now rich only in debts, a man who had let his father's substantial inheritance of over three million *sestertii* run through his fingers.

So the document tells us a lot about fortunes. Let us move on to "donatives," a form of more or less voluntary "taxation" which, during the golden years of empire, played a major part in ruining more than one of the richest provincial families.

When her son Pontianus married just before the Sabratha trial, Pudentilla alone had spent 50,000 *sestertii* on *sportulae* (gifts) for the people of Oea, not an insignificant sum to give away. Indeed, Apuleius asserted that he and his future wife decided to celebrate their own marriage in a villa on the outskirts of town precisely in order to avoid spending another 50,000 *sestertii*. In fact 60,000 *sestertii* would buy a moderately sized small-holding with an established produce yield. The same amount would have bought up to 60 *iugera* (15 hectares, or 37 acres) of fallow land, as we know from a Cyrenean inscription dating from the Flavian period.

A few more details. The whole of Oea knew that Herennius Rufinus and Sicinius Aemilianus had bribed their witness Junius Crassus, a man who also came from a good family but was a known glutton and an inveterate drunkard. They slipped him 3,000 *sestertii* – not a huge amount of money for lying at a trial involving the death penalty. But for many of those attending the hearing, such an amount was not in the least negligible. Lastly, we can add that when Pontianus died he showed how much he resented his wife, Herennius' daughter, by leaving her just 200 *denarii* (in other words 800 *sestertii*) in linen!

As we have seen, the *Apologia* contains a set of facts which, by linking them to real events, gives us a fairly accurate feel for the wealth enjoyed by the most notable provincial families in proconsular Africa during the Antonine age. The children of these families studied in Rome and Athens and aspired to make their débuts in Carthage. And when they were not busy in the capital of the empire, they could practically hold the whole of the political and cultural life of the province in the palm of their hand.

Notes

Tripolitania

1. Roughly equivalent to modern Fezzan; the largest human settlement was along the banks of the Wadi el-Agial where, in Roman times, the capital of the Garamantes stood. This was Garama, now known as Djerma.

2. In late Roman times Lepcis Minus, in modern-day Tunisia, straddled two provinces: Byzacium, which bordered Tripolitania, and Zengitana, whose capital was Carthage.

3. The Jebel is a rocky plateau to the north from which the wide pre-Saharan region falls away. The plateau contains the Gefara plain, an arc which touches the coast at Gabès in Tunisia, 18 kilometers (11.2 miles) west of Lepcis Magna.

4. The modern Wadi Caam, the only all-year watercourse in Tripolitania which flows out into the Mediterranean about 20 kilometers (12.4 miles) east of Lepcis.

5. I am using the term Emporia to refer exclusively to Lepcis, Oea, and Sabratha, even though in Polibius and Titus Livius the Emporia region seems to extend toward Tunisia and include a far wider area than that belonging to the three cities alone. Nonetheless, in Roman times these three cities remained the most important in the region and under Diocletian's reforms they became the *provincia Tripolitana*, the "province of three cities."

6. Using this as source material, the great Stephane Gsell and many scholars after him have ascribed the date when Lepcis was founded to at least around the beginning of the first millenium.

7. Under Italian rule the border between Cyrenaica and Tripolitania was brought into prominence at the site of the Arae Philaenorum (Ras el-Aali) when the Italian writer and politician Italo Balbo (1789–1853) built a monumental arch on the coast road which bore his name.

8 A division of the *populus* for electoral-religious purposes. The Roman term also covers the older Carthaginian institution.

9. and 10. *Inscriptions of Roman Tripolitania*, edited by J. Ward-Perkins and J. B. Reynolds (1952).

11. Inscription number 6 in *Inscriptions of Roman Tripolitania* edited by J. B. Ward-Perkins and J. Reynolds (1952).

12. G. Garbini, R *flessioni sul 'segno di Tanit'* [Reflections on the symbol of Tanit], in ιv φιλιας Χαριω. Miscellaea Eugenio Manni III, Rome, 1980. Garbini's comments are among the most profound I have read on the subject.

13. M. Rossi and G. Garbini, *Nuovi documenti epigrafici dalla Tripolitania romana* [New epigraphical documents on Roman Tripolitania], in *Libya Antiqua* 13–14, 1976–77 (1982).

14. P. A. Février, *Religion et domination dans l'Afrique romaine* [Religion and domination in Roman Africa], in *Dialogues d'Histoire ancienne*, 2, 1976 (Lit. Annals of University of Besançon 188).

Sabratha

1. To make the study of the remains of the city easier, J. P. Ward-Perkins divided them into *regiones* and *insulae*, as had been done for Pompeii and Ostia. The blocks of the VI *regio*, to the south of the Byzantine walls, are not shown in the maps that have been published using these divisions. This is because it was only after their publication that excavation work was begun in the area by E. Vergara Caffarelli and, to a lesser extent, by myself.

2. These are known as the "Office" Baths because they lie directly to the south of the offices used by the Italian excavation team.

Appendix

1. It seems unlikely that the farmland was 160 kilometers (100 miles) inland (which was already semidesert) or westward (in other words, toward Byzacena). What is more probable is that Pudentilla's estates lay about 100 kilometers (60 miles) to the other side of Oea, possibly in Lepcitian territory. In this context, remember that when Apuleius was unexpectedly accused of practicing magic, he was in Sabratha to represent his wife in commercial litigation against the Granii (*Apologia* 1, 5). Quite a number of this family are commemorated in Lepcitian epigraphs.

2. In fact it was a perfectly respectable dowry when you consider that 400,000 *sestertii* was the sum required to gain access to the equestrian order.

Forum at Lepcis at the beginning of the 3rd century A.D.

1. Temple with porticoed courtyard (start of 3rd century A.D.)
2. Public building with portico (middle of 3rd century A.D.)
3. Temple of Bacchus (Roman name of the Punic god Shadrapa)
4. Temple of Rome and Augustus
5. Platform for orators
6. Temple of Hercules (Roman name of the Punic god Milk'astart)
7. Engraved cartouche commemorating the paving of the forum under the proconsul Pison (5 B.C.–A.D. 2)
8. Semicircular stone bench (exedra), known as the Severan bench (start of 3rd century A.D.)
9. Temple of Cybele in a porticoed courtyard
10. Judicial Basilica used for public debates
11. Curia (meeting room for public assemblies)
12. Street leading to port
13. Cardo (street on main northeast/southwest axis of the town)

The origins of Lepcis

The city of Lepcis was founded by people from Tyre who ... had been forced out of their homeland by civil strife; so they crossed the sea and established themselves in these parts ... at the far end of Africa ... Over the years only the language spoken by the inhabitants of Lepcis changed, following intermarrying with the Numidians; for the most part, the laws and customs remained as those of Tyre; it was reasonably easy to maintain this here as they were far away from royal authority; between them and the more populated part of Numidia, there were vast stretches of desert.

Sallust, *The History of the Jurgurthine War*

The circus and amphitheater just outside Lepcis. Chariot races were held in the circus, gladiatorial fights in the amphitheater, and both attracted huge crowds.

An artist's impression of the Hadrians Baths in Lepcis.

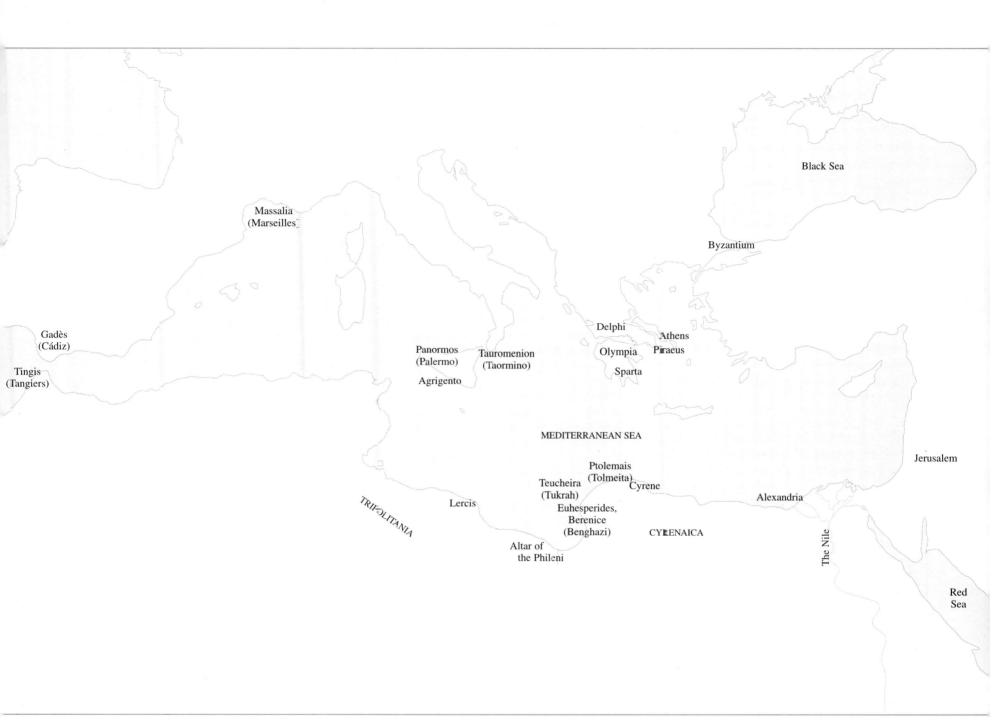

Black Sea

Massalia
(Marseilles)

Byzantium

Gadès
(Cádiz)

Delphi

Athens

Tingis
(Tangiers)

Panormos
(Palermo)

Tauromenion
(Taormino)

Olympia

Piraeus

Sparta

Agrigento

MEDITERRANEAN SEA

Jerusalem

Ptolemais
(Tolmeita)

Teucheira
(Tukrah)

Cyrene

Lercis

Alexandria

TRIPOLITANIA

Euhesperides,
Berenice
(Benghazi)

CYRENAICA

The Nile

Altar of
the Phileni

Red
Sea

Table of contents